What was the Continental Congress?

US History Textbook

Children's American History

Speedy Publishing LLC

40 E. Main St. #1156

Newark, DE 19711

www.speedypublishing.com

Copyright 2017

The Continental Congress consisted of a meeting of delegates from each of the thirteen American colonies.

During the Revolutionary War, they also served as the government. They were also called the Philadelphia Congress.

Read further to learn about how it got started, and how it was a forefront to government as we know it today.
CHESTNUT ST

They met during three incarnations beginning 1774 through 1789. The original call was over issues concerning the blockade and the Intolerable Acts which penalized Massachusetts, and allowed Benjamin Franklin in 1774 to convince these colonies to create a representation body.

The yearly logs created by this Congress are referred to as "Resolutions, Acts and Orders of Congress" providing a daily account of the issues and debates.

Early on, the delegates were divided as to whether or not to depart from Crown rule. The second Continental Congress approved a resolution proclaiming independence, and no opposing vote was recorded.

Two days later, the Declaration of Independence was issued announcing themselves as a new nation known as the United States of America.

It established the Continental Army, giving command to George Washington. It waged a war with Great Britain, issued a treaty with France, and funded the war with loans and money.

The First Continental Congress convened September 5 to October 26, 1774. Except for Georgia, delegates from each colony met in Philadelphia, at Carpenter's Hall.

They talked about the state of affairs with Britain, as well as the Intolerable Acts, which British Parliament had levied on Boston as reprimand for its Boston Tea Party.

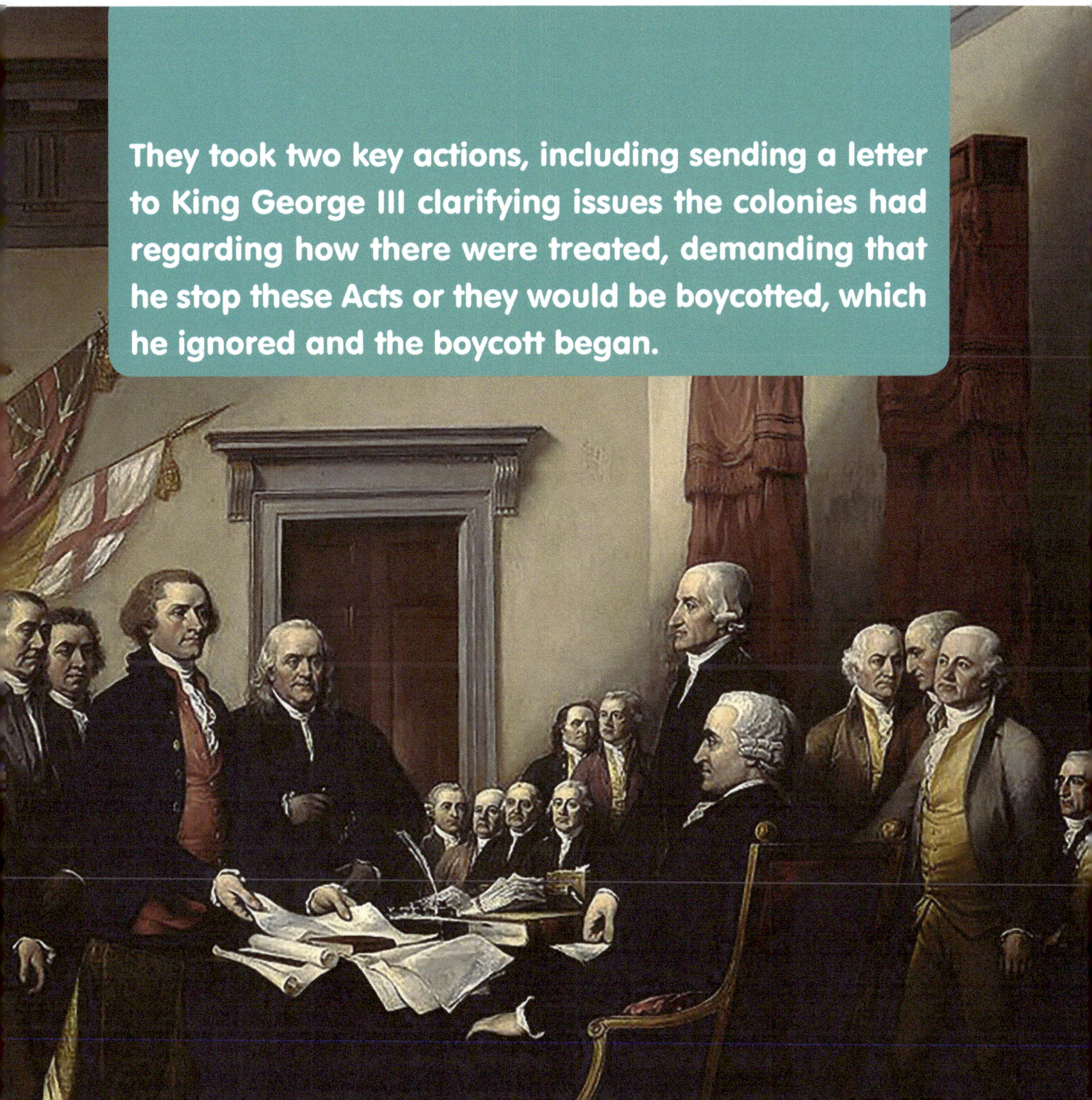

They took two key actions, including sending a letter to King George III clarifying issues the colonies had regarding how there were treated, demanding that he stop these Acts or they would be boycotted, which he ignored and the boycott began.

They also developed a plan to again meet May of 1775 if British demands were not met.

George Washington, Patrick Henry, and John Adams were some of the members of the First Continental Congress. Its President was Peyton Rudolph.

In this Congress, a delegate of Virginia, Patrick Henry, declared "I am not a Virginian, I am an American".

On May 10, 1775, the Second Continental Congress met for the first time. The delegates then met in various sessions through March of 1781, when they ratified the Articles of Confederation.

They first met in Philadelphia at the State House, later referred to as Independence Hall.

They also held meetings in Maryland, Baltimore, and York, Pennsylvania. Different from the First Continental Congress, Georgia joined so all of the thirteen colonies were now represented.

With the beginning of the Revolutionary War including the battles of Lexington and Concord, much had occurred in the months prior to the end of First Continental Congress.

Congress had to urgently take care of some business including the formation of an army.

The colonies of St. John's Island, Nova Scotia and Quebec were invited to attend the Second Continental Congress, but did not show up.

The Continental Army was established on June 14, 1775 by the Second Continental Congress. George Washington was made General of this army.

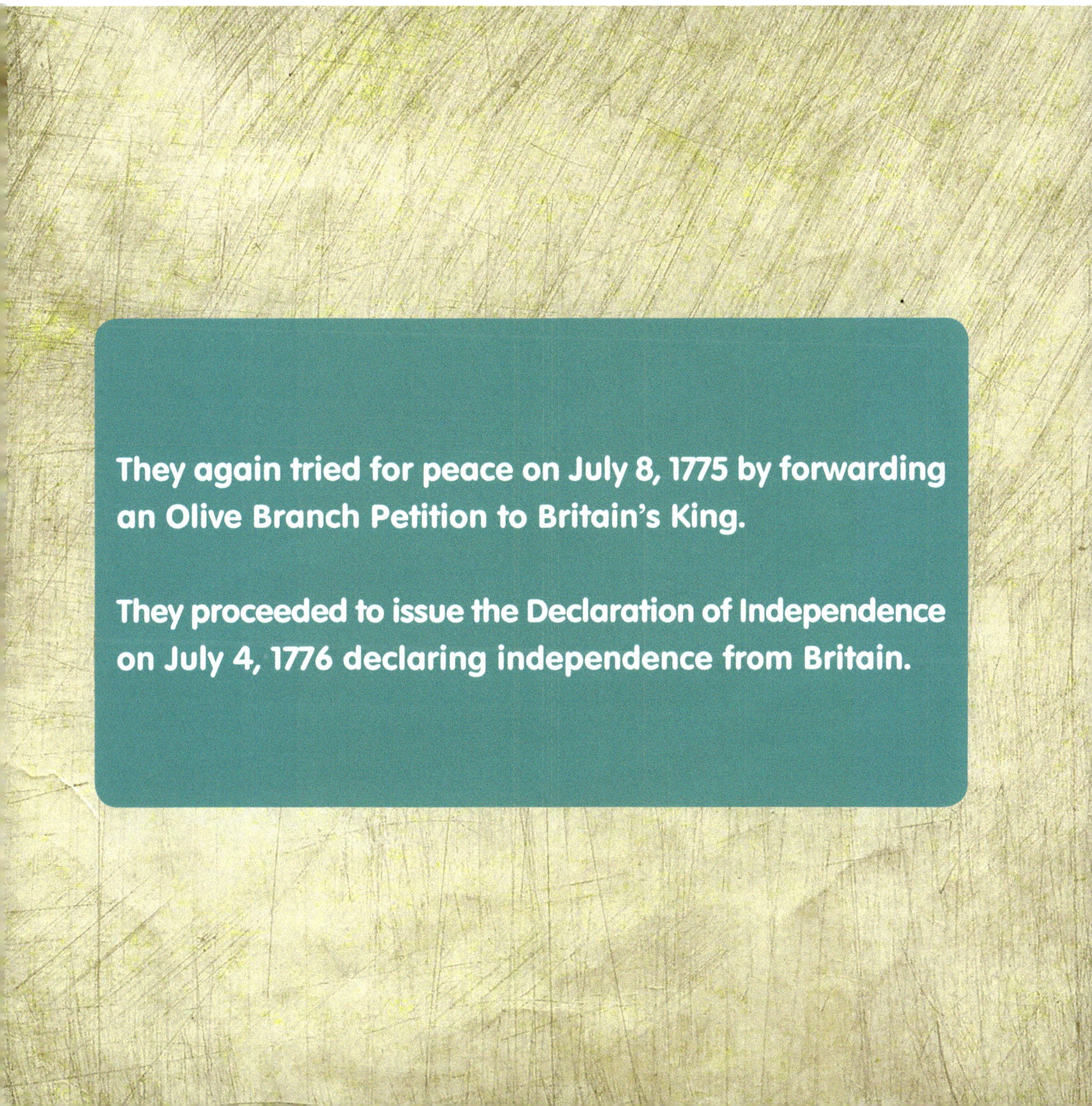
They again tried for peace on July 8, 1775 by forwarding an Olive Branch Petition to Britain's King.

They proceeded to issue the Declaration of Independence on July 4, 1776 declaring independence from Britain.

The Flag Resolution was passed on June 14, 1777, for the official flag of the United States.

The Articles of Confederation were signed March 1, 1781, creating a formal government. Congress then became known as the Congress of the Confederation.

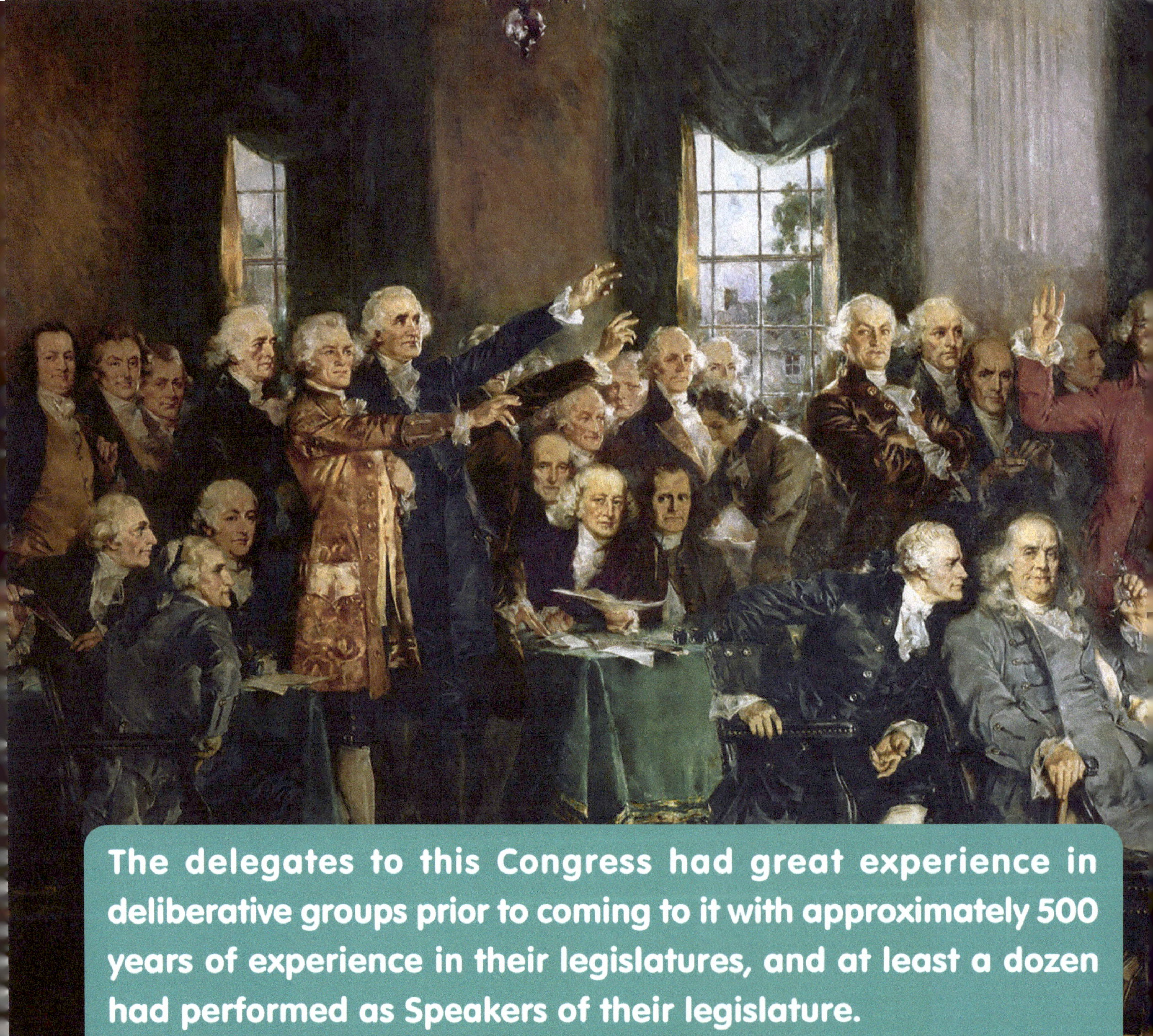

The delegates to this Congress had great experience in deliberative groups prior to coming to it with approximately 500 years of experience in their legislatures, and at least a dozen had performed as Speakers of their legislature.

The Great Britain Parliament and many of their Colonial groups had great Speakers and standing committees with powerful chairmen, and power held by the colonial Governor or the British Monarch.

The Continental Congress was based less, however on British Parliament or local state assemblies than the Stamp Act Congress, made up of nine colonies.

Of the 56 delegates, 9 that attended in 1774 previously had attended the Stamp Act Congress of 1765.

These delegates were some of the most well-respected. They influenced its direction from its opening, at what time decisions were made on procedures and organization, and made it over 14 years when the Congress adjourned on March 2, 1788.

The delegates selected a President of the Continental Congress to watch over the debate, keep order, and confirm that journals were maintained and letters and documents be delivered and published.

The President would otherwise have little power, and be mostly a figurehead only used to greet visiting dignitaries: this office became less powerful and more honorable.

The job was then not really sought or retained for very long: in 14 years, there were 16 presidents.

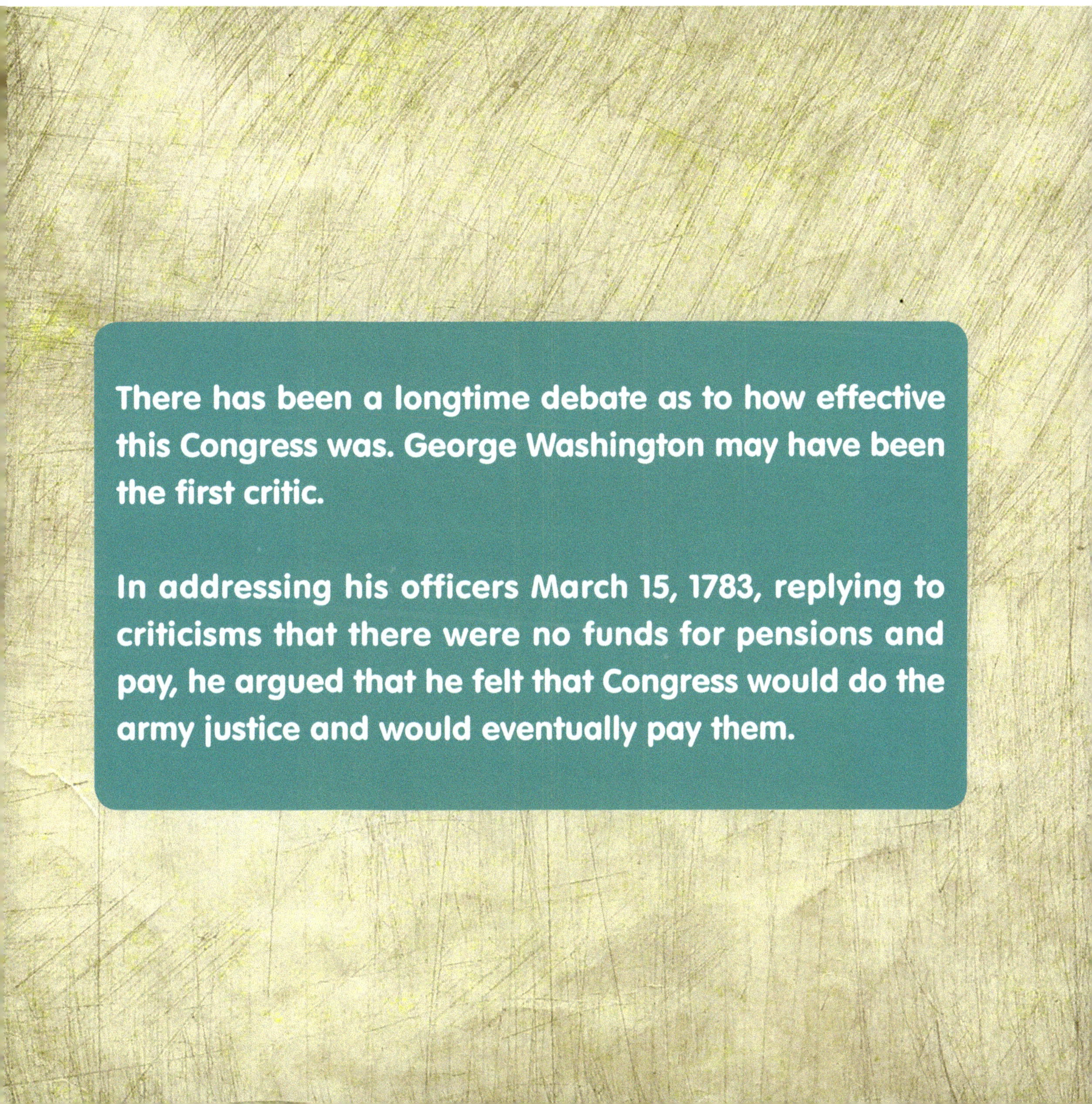

There has been a longtime debate as to how effective this Congress was. George Washington may have been the first critic.

In addressing his officers March 15, 1783, replying to criticisms that there were no funds for pensions and pay, he argued that he felt that Congress would do the army justice and would eventually pay them.

But he also advised that there were a variety of interests and deliberations could be slow.

The
Thirteen
Colonies
The United States was formed in 1776, from the thirteen British colonies. Many had been around for over 100 years, including Virginia, founded in 1607.

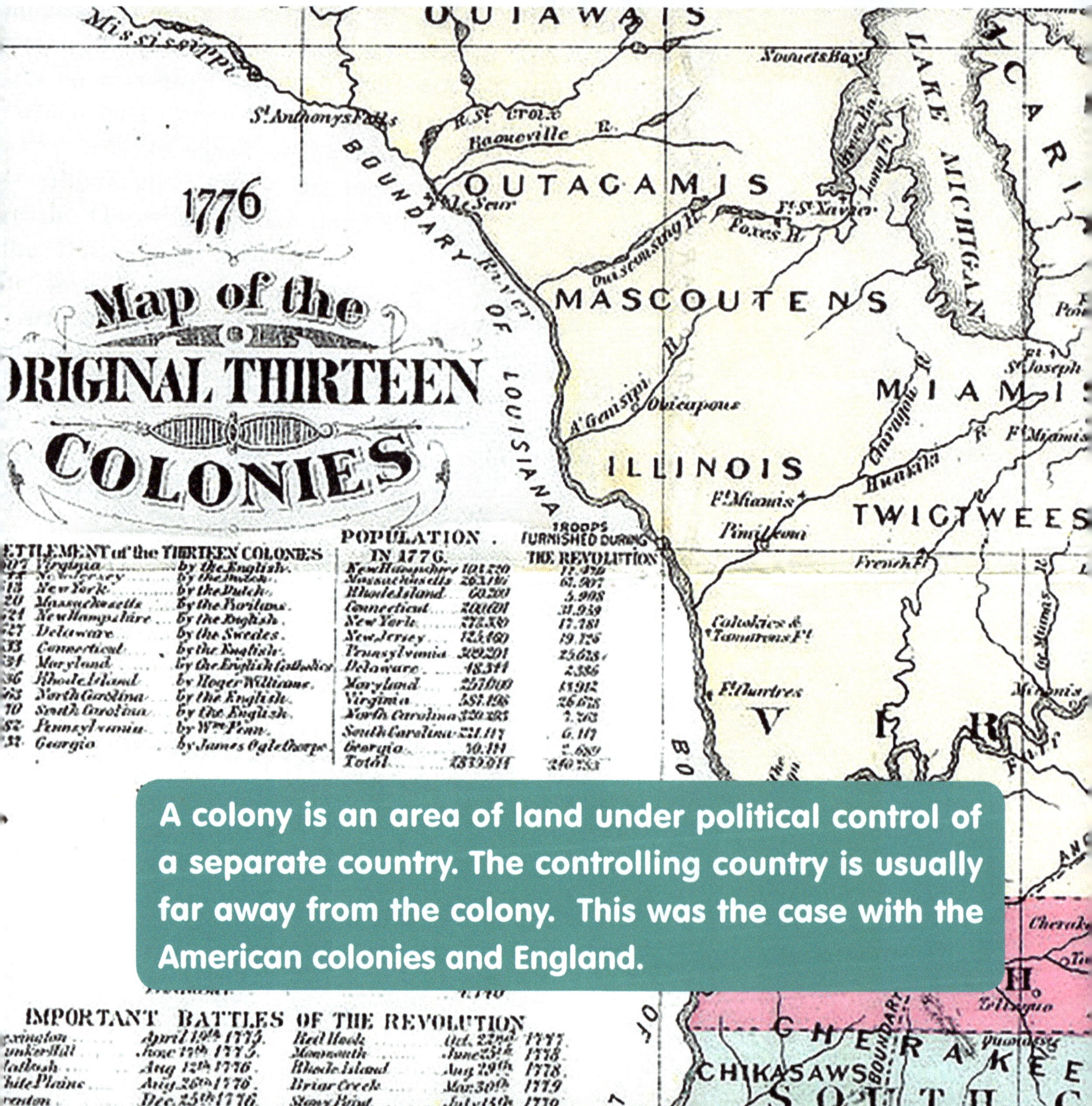

A colony is an area of land under political control of a separate country. The controlling country is usually far away from the colony. This was the case with the American colonies and England.

HURONS LAKE
CANADA
LAKE ONTARIO
LAKE ERIE
Ft Pelee
Long Pt
Niagara Fall
Oswego
Onondaga
Iroquois
BOUNDARY
Ft St Johns
Lake Champlain
Crown Point
Ft Frederick
Ticonderoga
Lake George
Ft Edward
Saratoga
Albany
NEW HAMPSHIRE
NEW ENGLAND
MASSACHUSETTS
Boston
CONNECTICUT
RHODE ISLAND
Newhaven
Hudson R.
Martha's Vineyard
Nantucket I. & Shoals
Cape Cod
Cape Cod Bay
CONFEDERATE
PENNSYLVANIA
Venango
Onondaga
Wyoming
Shamokin
Ft Shamokin
Granville Ft
Pittsburg
Fort Pitt
Bedford
Logs Town
Kuskusking
Wiokeck Ft
Reading Ft
Easton
Bethlehem
Germantown
Philadelphia
NEW YORK
Amboy
NEW JERSEY
Gloucester
Newark
Burlington
Perth Amboy
Staten Island
Long Island
Charlestown
Shrewsbury
Beach Isle
Barnegat Beach
Little Egg Harbor
Great Egg Harbor
C. May
C. Hinlopen
False Cape
Cedar Isles
MARYLAND
DELAWARE
Winchester
Alexandria
Annapolis
Fredericksburg
York R.
VIRGINIA
FRENCH
BOUNDARY
ALLEGHANY
THE BLUE RIDGE
James R.
Richmond
Williamsburg
Jamestown
Yorktown
Norfolk
Suffolk
C. Charles
C. Henry
Roanoke R.
Currituck Inlet
Edenton
Roanoke Inlet
Albemarle Sound
CAROLINA
Bath Town
Roanoke Isle
C. Hatteras
New Berne
Bradford
C. Lookout
Ocracoke Inlet
Welsh Settlements
Catawba
Keowee
Swansea Co
ATLANTIC OCEAN
boundary on the sea coast of the United States

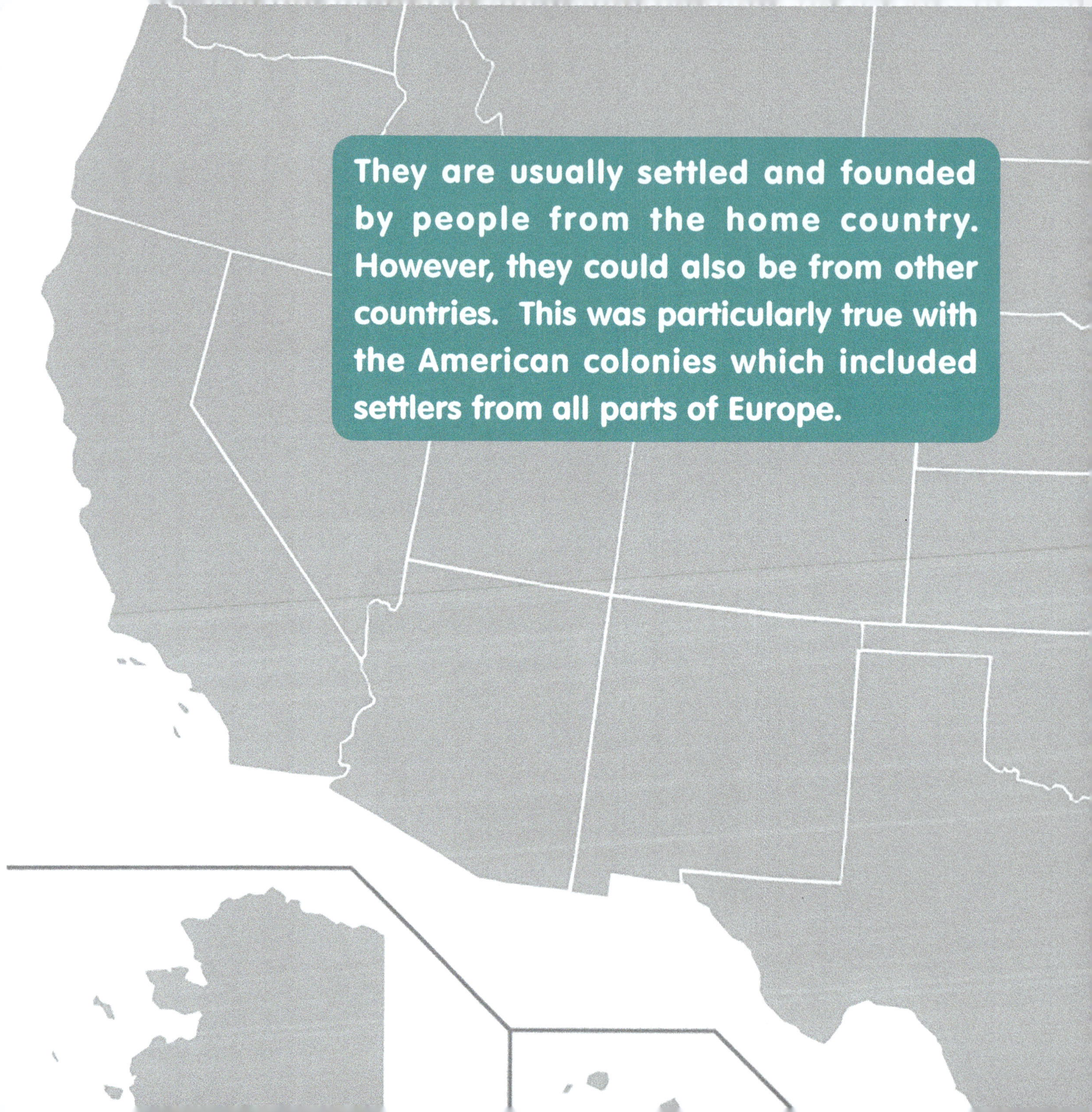

They are usually settled and founded by people from the home country. However, they could also be from other countries. This was particularly true with the American colonies which included settlers from all parts of Europe.

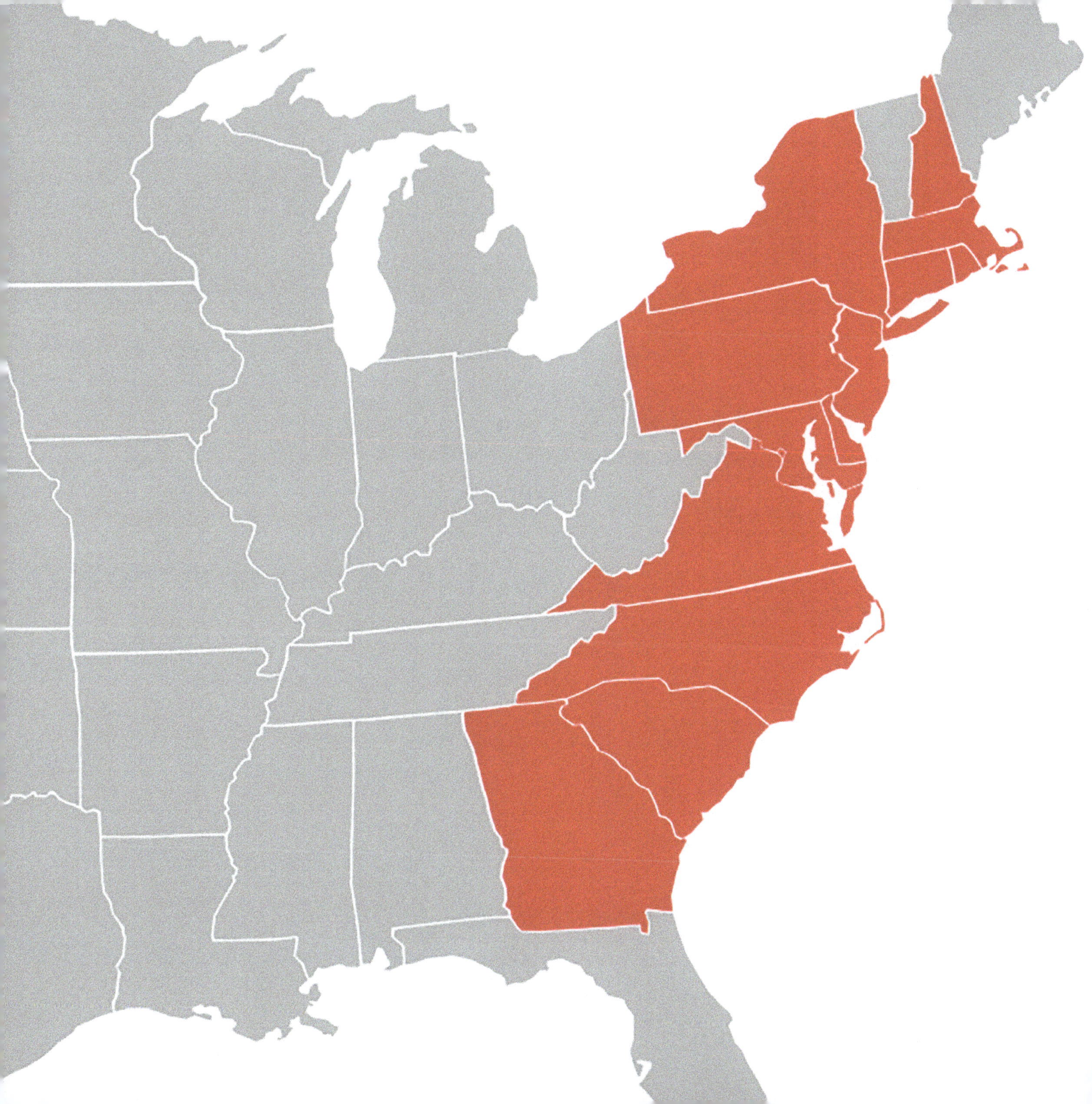

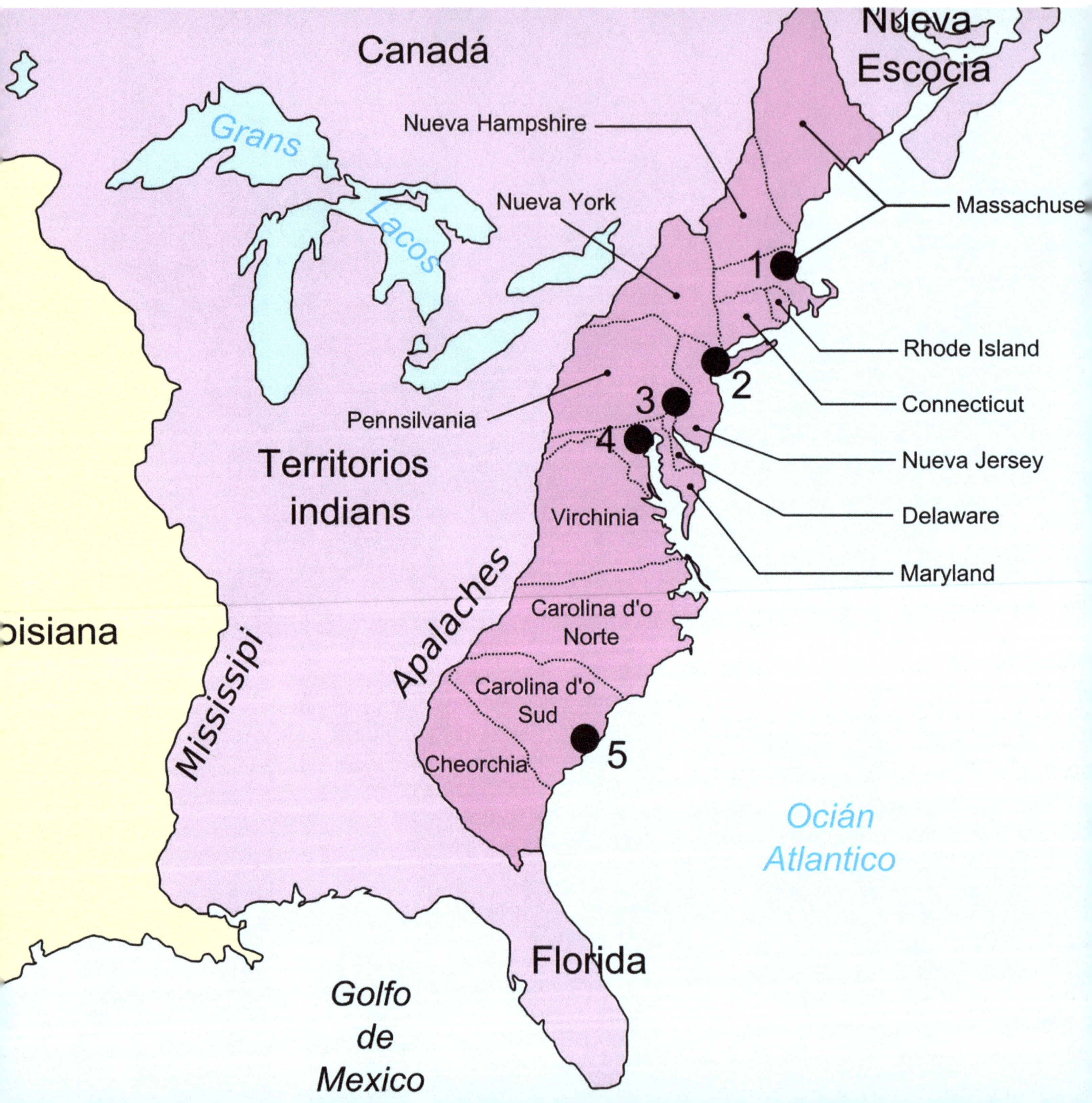

Canadá
Nueva Escocia
Grans Lacos
Nueva Hampshire
Nueva York
Massachuse
Rhode Island
Connecticut
Nueva Jersey
Delaware
Maryland
Pennsilvania
Territorios indians
Apalaches
Virchinia
Carolina d'o Norte
Carolina d'o Sud
Cheorchia
Mississipi
bisiana
Florida
Golfo de Mexico
Ocián Atlantico
1
2
3
4
5

The thirteen colonies include Virginia, founded in 1607, by John Smith and the London Company, New York, founded in 1626, originally established by the Dutch but later becoming a British colony in 1664, New Hampshire, founded in 1625 by John Mason, Massachusetts Bay, founded in 1630 by John Wheelright, Maryland, founded in 1633 by George and Cecil Calvert which became a safe place for Catholics, Connecticut, founded in 1636 by Thomas Hooker when he had to leave Massachusetts, Rhode Island founded in 1636 by Roger Williams, Delaware, founded in 1638 by Peter Minuit with New Sweden Company, North Carolina, founded in 1663, which was a part of Province of Carolina originally, South Carolina, founded in 1663 was part of Province of Carolina originally, splitting off North Carolina in 1712, New Jersey, founded in 1664, was originally settled by the Dutch, and the English overtook in 1664, and Pennsylvania, founded in 1681 by William Penn along with the Quakers, Georgia, founded in 1732 by James Olethorpe.

Queen Elizabeth

Why were these colonies established? In order to expand her British empire and counter the Spanish, Queen Elizabeth wanted to establish the colonies.

They thought they would create new jobs, find wealth, and establish ports for trade along the coast. However, each colony had its own history about its discovery. Several were founded by religious leaders or people looking for freedom with their religion.

Canadá
Nueva
Escocia
Grandes
Lagos
Nueva Hampshire
Nueva York
Massachuset
1
Rhode Island
Territorio
indio
3
2
Connecticut
Pensilvania
4
Nueva Jersey
Delaware
Maryland
Misisipí
Virginia
Apalaches
Carolina del
Norte
Carolina del
Sur
5
Georgia
Océano
Atlántico

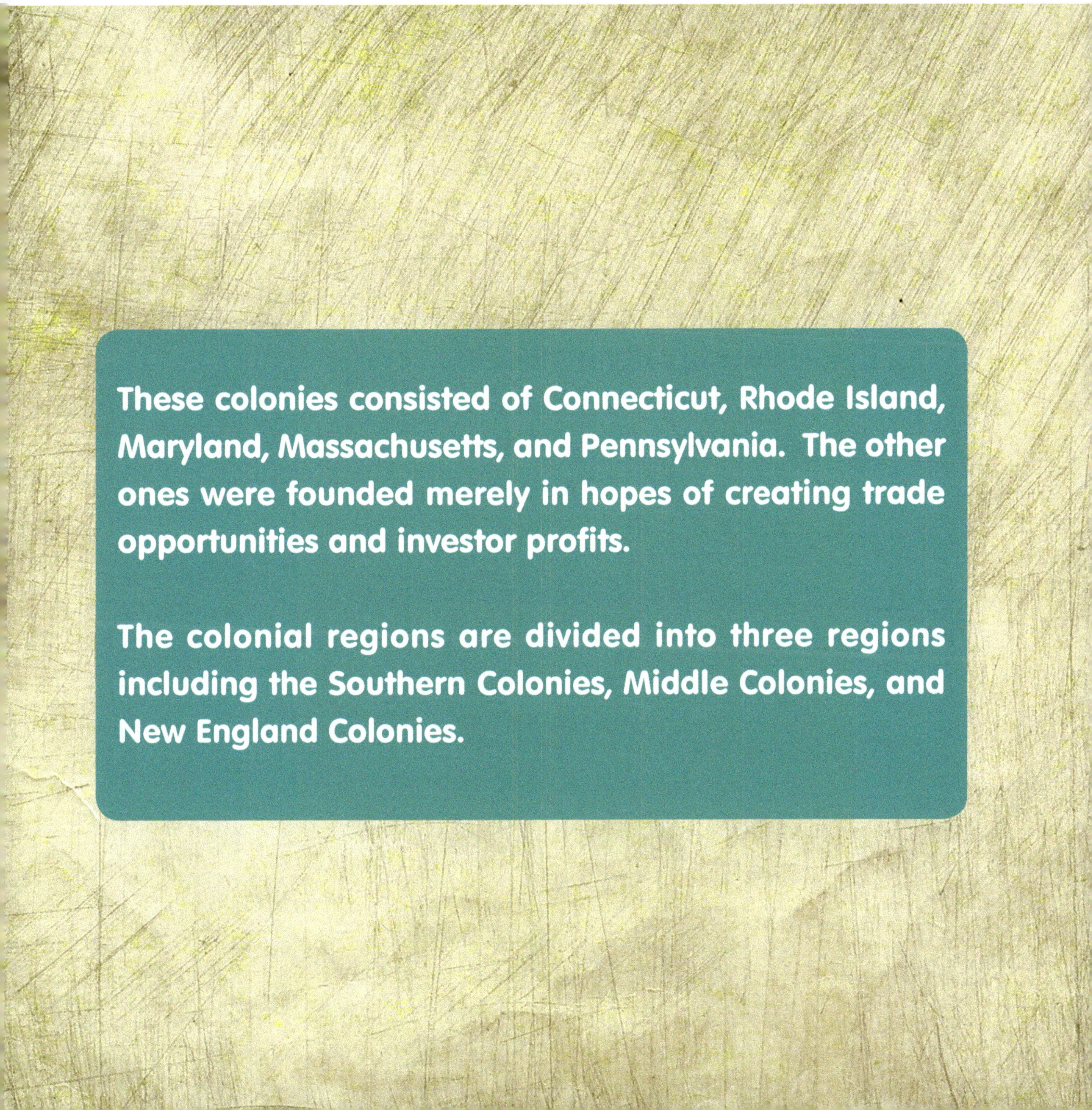

These colonies consisted of Connecticut, Rhode Island, Maryland, Massachusetts, and Pennsylvania. The other ones were founded merely in hopes of creating trade opportunities and investor profits.

The colonial regions are divided into three regions including the Southern Colonies, Middle Colonies, and New England Colonies.

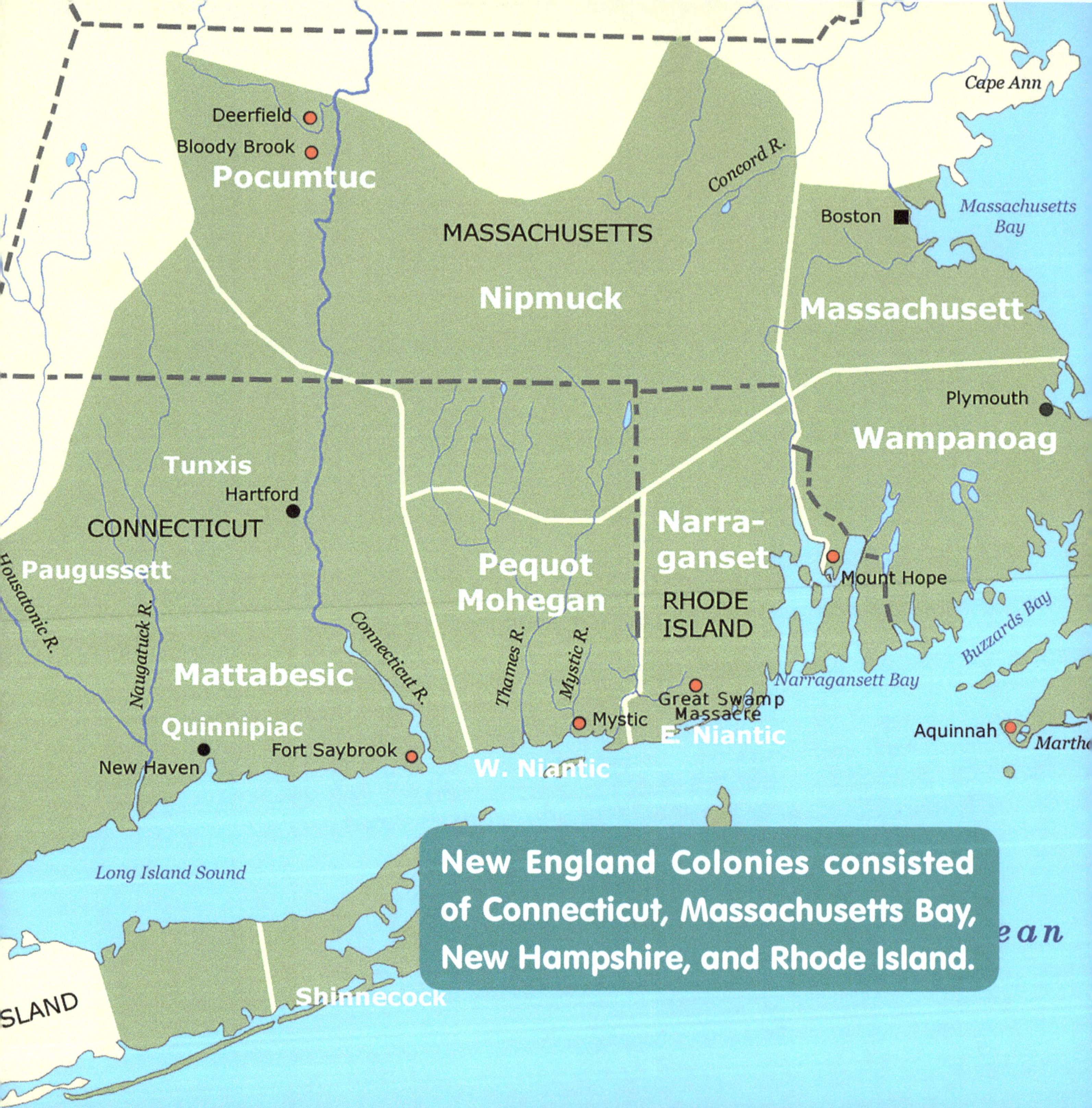

Cape Ann
Deerfield
Bloody Brook
Pocumtuc
Concord R.
MASSACHUSETTS
Massachusetts Bay
Boston
Nipmuck
Massachusett
Plymouth
Wampanoag
Tunxis
Hartford
CONNECTICUT
Narra-ganset
Paugussett
Housatonic R.
Naugatuck R.
Connecticut R.
Pequot Mohegan
RHODE ISLAND
Mount Hope
Buzzards Bay
Mattabesic
Thames R.
Mystic R.
Great Swamp Massacre
Narragansett Bay
Quinnipiac
Mystic
E. Niantic
Aquinnah
Martha
New Haven
Fort Saybrook
W. Niantic
Long Island Sound
ean
SLAND
Shinnecock

New England Colonies consisted of Connecticut, Massachusetts Bay, New Hampshire, and Rhode Island.

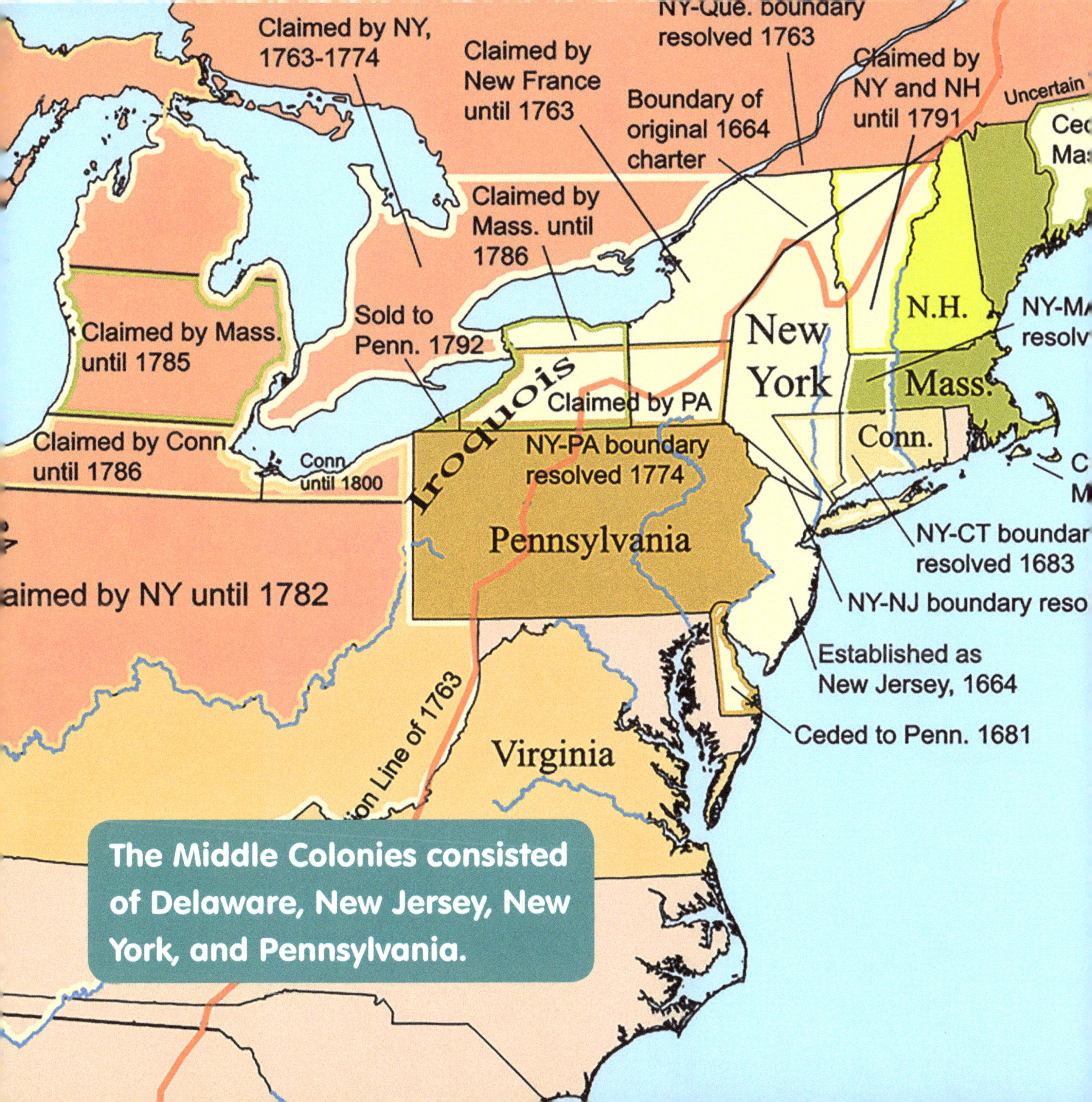

Claimed by NY, 1763-1774
Claimed by New France until 1763
NY-Que. boundary resolved 1763
Boundary of original 1664 charter
Claimed by NY and NH until 1791
Uncertain
Ceded Mas
Claimed by Mass. until 1786
Claimed by Mass. until 1785
Sold to Penn. 1792
N.H.
NY-MA resolv
New York
Claimed by Conn until 1786
Conn until 1800
Iroquois
Claimed by PA
NY-PA boundary resolved 1774
Mass.
Conn.
C M
Claimed by NY until 1782
Pennsylvania
NY-CT boundar resolved 1683
NY-NJ boundary reso
Established as New Jersey, 1664
Ceded to Penn. 1681
on Line of 1763
Virginia
The Middle Colonies consisted of Delaware, New Jersey, New York, and Pennsylvania.

The Southern Colonies consisted of Georgia, Maryland, North Carolina, South Carolina, and Virginia.

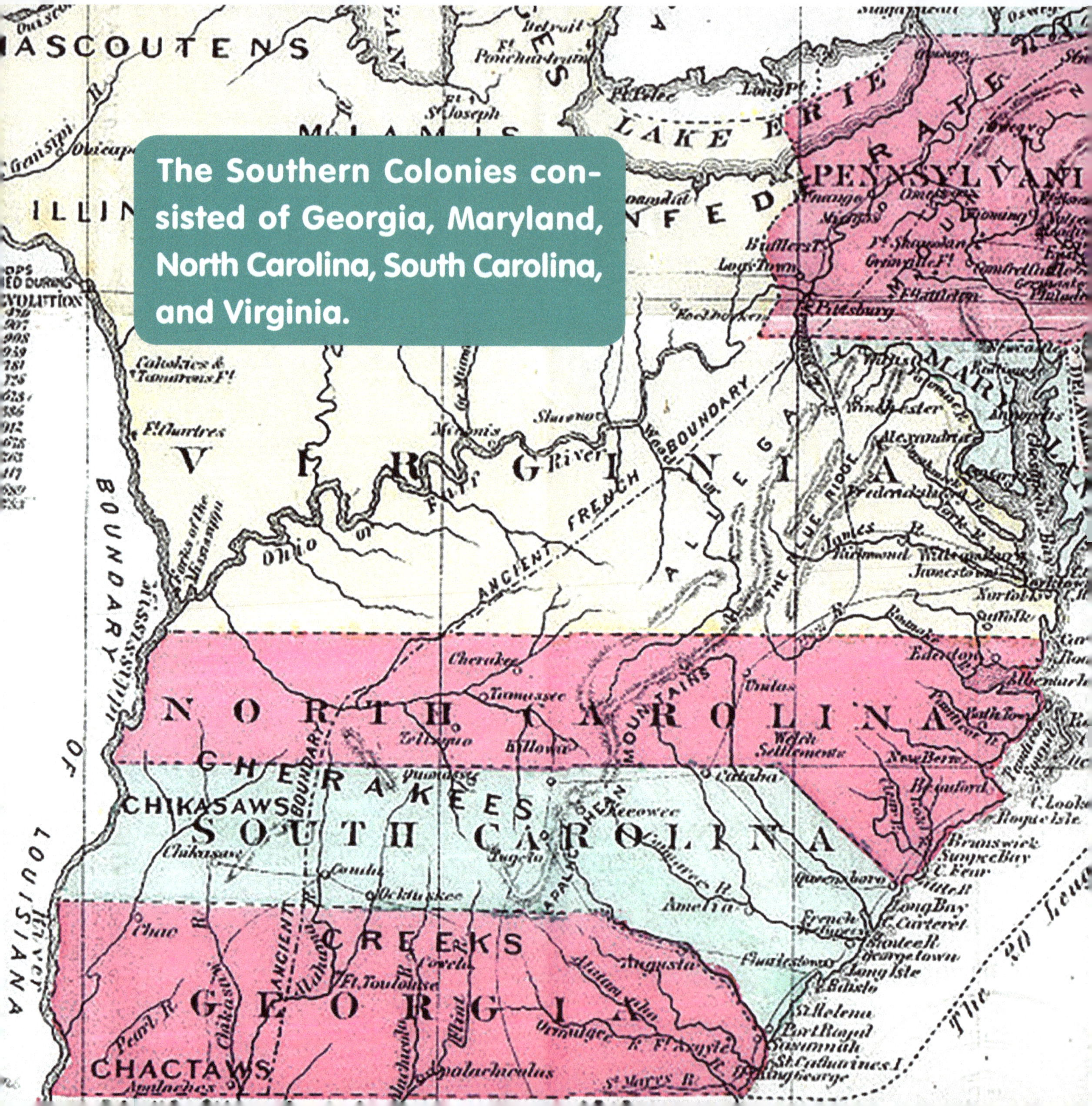

Can you imagine a turkey as the symbol representing the United States? It could have happened if Ben Franklin had his way.

THOMAS JEFFERSON
He wanted our symbol to be the turkey. However, Thomas Jefferson and John Adams thought the bald eagle would be a better option.

JOHN ADAMS

Many commentators believe that the leaderless, slow, weak, and small-committee driven, congress a failure, largely due to the fact that at the end of the war the Articles of Confederation were no longer suitable for the needs of a peaceful nation, and that it should, following Madison's suggestions, be called for revision and replacement of it.

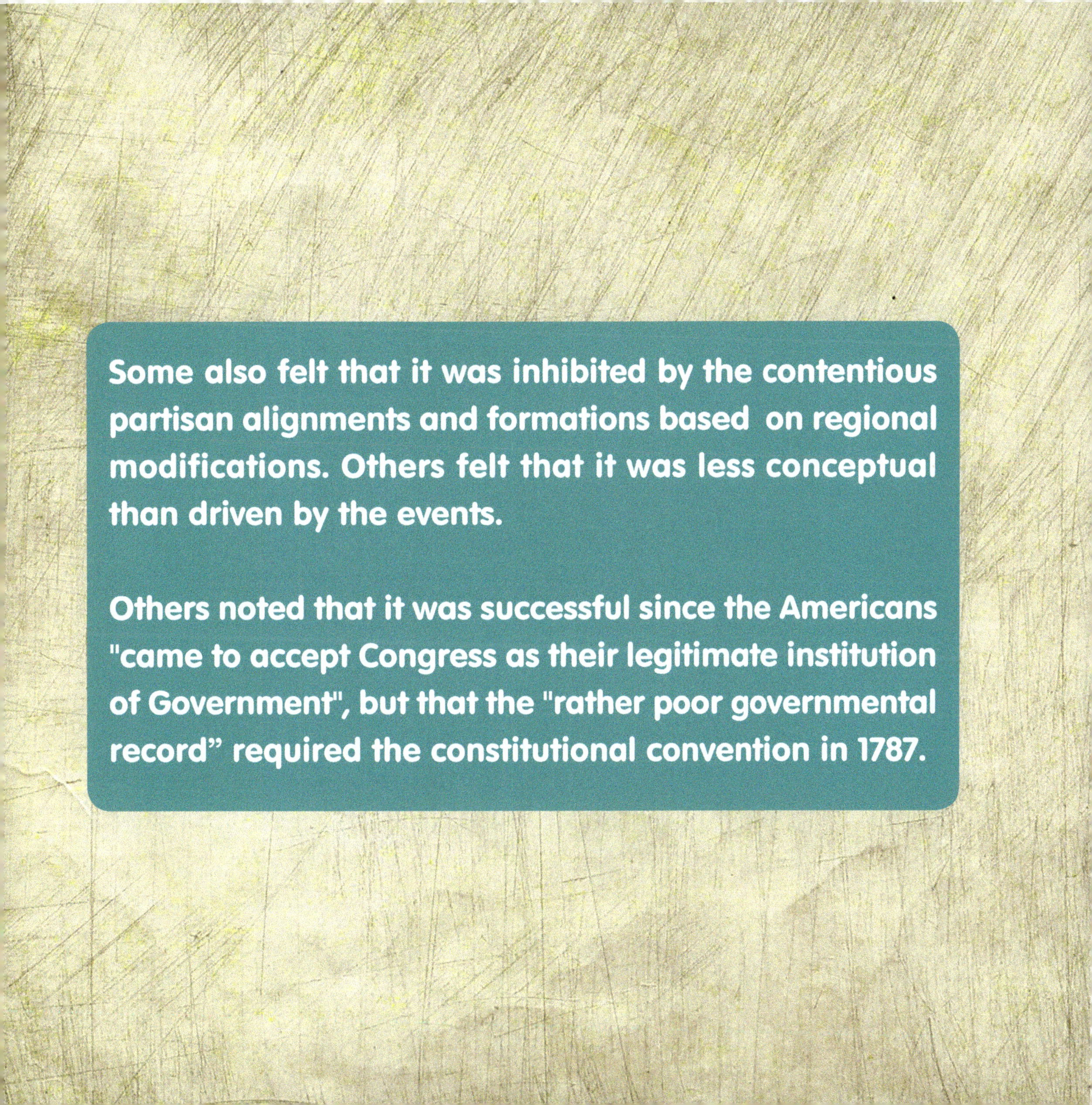

Some also felt that it was inhibited by the contentious partisan alignments and formations based on regional modifications. Others felt that it was less conceptual than driven by the events.

Others noted that it was successful since the Americans "came to accept Congress as their legitimate institution of Government", but that the "rather poor governmental record" required the constitutional convention in 1787.

Be sure to check out more interesting facts about the Continental Congress by researching the internet, going to your local library, or asking questions of your teachers, family, and friends.

Visit
BABY PROFESSOR
EDUCATION KIDS
www.BabyProfessorBooks.com
to download Free Baby Professor eBooks and view
our catalog of new and exciting Children's Books

9 798869 410313